Published by Caliaymee, LLC
California, U.S.A.
www.caliaymee.com

First Edition ♡

ISBN: 979-8-9990944-1-4 (Paperback edition)

Printed and published independently in the United States.

For the version of
me that never gave up.
For the people who
cracked me open.
And for anyone still
trying to break free—
This one's for you.

WTF is Self-Sabotage

It's the invisible force that blocks the life you say you want.

It convinces you that staying small is safer than stepping into your full potential.

Self-sabotage looks like **procrastination**—binge-watching Netflix or doom-scrolling while your to-do list glares at you.

It's **overthinking**—replaying every conversation and wondering what you should've, could've, or would've said.

It's **perfectionism**—waiting for the "perfect" time to start. *Spoiler: it never shows up.*

It's **people-pleasing**—putting everyone else first until you forget who the hell you are.

It's choosing **shitty situations** out of fear and familiarity instead of leaping into the unknown.

It shows up as **dimming** your potential, convincing yourself you're not ready, not good enough.

But it's not a weakness—it's a protection strategy.

One that comes with a shady price tag:
Your freedom, your joy, your growth.

Most of us don't even realize we're doing it.

We get stuck in cycles of comfort and routine, avoiding the "pain-in-the-ass" feelings that change might stir up.

But here's the truth:
Self-sabotage isn't permanent. The moment you recognize it, you start taking your life back.

Awareness is the first step.

The next step?
Turning the page...

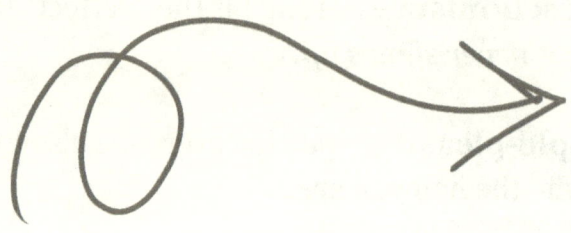

You can't change what you're not aware of.

Welcome to Real Talk

Ditching Patterns, Truth Bombs, and Blowing Up Old Bullshit

This is your wake-up-and-do-something moment.

A kick-in the-ass call to finally stop the bullshit and break free from the shit that's been dragging you down.

Amy's dropping unfiltered truths on burnout, perfectionism, fear-in disguise, and those shady little ways self-sabotage shows up to wreck your vibe
—whether it's at work, in your relationships, or just life in general.

Packed with truth bombs, real talk, and zero fluff, her book helps you name your patterns, break your cycles, and step into a life that actually feels good
—on your damn terms.

This is the first in her series of tell-it-like-it-is books designed to help you step into a life that actually feels good
—for good.

That's where this book comes in and blows that shit up —with lots of love, sass and a whole lotta truth.

Chapter One

Self-Sabotage Doesn't Always Make a Grand Entrance

Sometimes, It Wears Yoga Pants and Looks Like a TON of Productivity

Self-sabotage doesn't always scream and cuss at you.

Sometimes, it shows up in your most *"productive"* moments, **pretending** to be a badge of honor.

At first, I thought I was crushing it—pure ambition.

But in reality? I was sinking. ***Fast.***

Later, I realized it was fear... disguised as a job title.

I was working endless hours—at least 12 a day, sometimes more. I'd get up at 3 or 4 in the morning, drag myself out of bed with four hours of sleep, and clock in by 5:30.

I'd work until dark, thinking I was helping and doing the right thing.

But all I was really doing was burning out and *forgetting to include myself in the equation.*

I was pushing to prove my value and dedication to management—working myself into the ground like a fucking machine just to show I could get the job done.

And my body?
It was waving a white flag.

Constant headaches, insomnia, barely eating, overthinking, and running on fumes just to make it through the day.

But here's the kicker:
The jobs I held throughout my corporate America "career" were impossible for one person. Let alone two or three.

I kept trying to out perform a toxic system, thinking if I just did better, it would love me back.

Shocker:
It never did. Not once. Not ever.

Burnout doesn't give you awards or recognition.

It gives you exhaustion, resentment, and a gut-deep level knowing that something's gotta change.

For me, it wasn't just the hours. It was the way I refused to ask for help. The way I tied my survival to staying useful.

Here's the thing about self-sabotage—it hides behind what looks like **"productivity."**

I never asked for help. With anything.

I was terrified, and convinced myself I had to take on the world alone. So I kept grinding. And grinding. I wasn't just working to make ends meet. I was working to make everyone else proud.

But the truth? I couldn't even be proud of myself.

Not yet.

But deep down, I knew I deserved better.

And that fear of letting go? ***It had to stop.***

The corporate America environments I worked in were toxic.

But I didn't see it at the time. My people-pleasing bullshit took over. I said yes to everything, took on too much, and got stuck in the cycle of making everyone else comfortable.

What was I given in return?
More work and toxic, micromanaged "support" gassing up
my overworked, superhero status to get 'er done.

For most of my career, I thought success meant sitting
behind a desk, playing with numbers, and sending emails.
But deep down, I knew I was made for more.

I wanted to help people
—not survive inside a broken system.

When I was laid off, I finally saw the truth. It was time to
walk away from the chaos.

When one door closes, another one opens—*and I was done*
being treated like I was disposable.

So, what was really going on here? **Perfectionism**.

I thought I had to over perform to prove my value. To
support myself. To keep everyone else happy.

But here's the truth:
—the fear of showing up for myself, fear of asking for help,
fear of saying, "What do I need?"—that was the real driver.

And that fear? *It had to stop—once and for all.*

For years, I hit wall after wall. Every corner I turned, there
was resistance. People. Departments. Situations.

Resistance coming at me from all angles.

But resistance isn't failure—**it's redirection.**
It's your higher self whispering, *"This ain't it, babe"*

If you're feeling resistance: blocked, rejected, or stuck, it's not a roadblock.

It's a message:
Your energy isn't meant to go that way.
Once I got out of my own way? *Everything started to flow.*

**Where your attention goes
—your intention will flow.**

I finally got it.

The last puzzle piece clicked when I was laid off. That was the wake-up call. After over 40 years of chasing worth and validation in all the wrong places, I saw clearly.
—I had to course-correct.

I had to figure out what the hell I actually wanted. Who I was. And how I was going to make it happen.

So, I started an overhaul. I looked at how to build a better foundation.

And I celebrated every empowering step I took.
—even if I couldn't see the results yet.

I changed my thoughts. My habits. My routines. My strategies. Even how I ate. I stopped listening to all the noise around me—including shutting down my social media and turning the damn TV off.

If this sounds familiar, good.

Not because you deserve the burnout.
But because awareness is the first step to change.

You are not broken.

You've just been on autopilot, running on patterns you never chose.

You have the right and the power to change that.

Right now.

And you damn well deserve it.

Burnout isn't a badge of honor.

It's a screaming check engine light you've been ignoring.

Pull. Over.

Chapter 2

Perfectionism

The Art of Self-Sabotage in a Dope Outfit

We all say we want to change. We throw those words around like we've got it all figured out. But let's be real— *most of us have at least one habit that's quietly screaming otherwise.*

For me? *Overthinking.*

I'd get stuck in the cycle of refining, tweaking, and fixing until I couldn't even see the opportunity staring me in the face.

I'd overdo it—polishing every damn detail, reworking everything until it felt "perfect".
—and the idea of being enough without all that extra bullshit?

Terrifying.

I thought that if I made things perfect enough, I'd finally feel ready.

Guess what? *I never did.*

I missed out on real opportunities because I was too busy trying to make everything flawless.

I'd bomb interviews because I couldn't stop overthinking.

Or I'd do great, but still feel like I came off as "too much" or "not enough"—*like I was trying way too hard to be perfect.*

I'd set new goals for myself, thinking I had it all figured out, only to freeze up because I wasn't sure how to make them happen—*even though deep down, I knew exactly what needed to be done.*

Side note...

follow your dreams

Have you ever found yourself envisioning big dreams and goals, but they feel so out of reach?

Check this out:
Just by thinking, you've already started creating and you are capable of making anything happen. Your dreams and goals are waiting for you—**what are you waiting for?**

You're not just daydreaming. Your mind is opening doors to opportunities you didn't even know existed—*also known as your potential.*

Change doesn't require everything to be perfectly planned.

It's not about having it all figured out. It's about committing to figuring it out as you go.

That's the key: *taking action even if it's imperfect.*

New habits? They don't just happen overnight.

It's not like they're going to magically appear because you decided you wanted to change your life.

They need time to marinate, sink in and become part of your new "norm".

You might feel uncomfortable and you may stumble from time to time—**But that discomfort?**

It's part of the process. *You're closer to a breakthrough than you think.*

So, when those ideas or visions of change come to mind, don't dismiss them as "impossible."

They're messages from your future self showing you it's already within your reach and potential.

The difference between feeling stuck and moving forward isn't about having every single detail figured out.

It's about making the choice to dive in, trusting you'll figure it out along the way.

It takes time to integrate new behaviors into your daily life.

Hell, your old habits didn't show up overnight, right? So, don't expect the new ones to either.

Change isn't easy.

You'll get pushback—*not just from people around you, but from yourself too.*

Change feels weird. It's unfamiliar. But you know what?

That's a good thing.

You have to get uncomfortable to grow or you'll continue seeking comfort in external "things" that are keeping you exactly where you are and don't want to be.

Anyone who's ever done something big has been uncomfortable AF while doing it.

I spent so much time overcommitting—saying "yes" to everything, thinking I could juggle it all and still keep my shit together.

I kept throwing more on my plate—*until my body literally* **forced me to stop.**

I was in **people-pleasing mode**—constantly trying to prove myself and be perfect in everyone's eyes.

But the reality?
I was fucking exhausted. Mentally, emotionally, and physically drained.

And the worst part? I was so focused on what wasn't working, I couldn't see all the good things that were already around me.

Here's the secret:
When you start focusing on what's working, everything changes.

Suddenly, you see all the good around you—*the stuff you took for granted. The things that were already there.*

That's it—that's the shift

You stop looking for what's wrong and start seeing what's right.

You stop seeking validation from outside sources and realize that you're already enough.

The world doesn't need to tell you that—you just need to remind yourself.

If something feels "weird" or "different," that's okay. **Embrace it.**

If you've found something that's working for you—a new habit, a new way of thinking, or a different approach, **stick with it.**

Even if it doesn't make sense to society or anyone else.

If it's helping you take better care of yourself and invest in your future moving forward, keep doing it.

If it's working for you, that's all that matters.

The most important lesson I learned is this:
You don't need anyone else's approval. Stop looking for it.

You sure AF don't need to prove anything to anyone else. **—and least of all to yourself.**

You've always been enough. You've always mattered.

In the past, I thought I had to earn validation—so I'd overcommit to projects, hoping that by pushing myself harder, I'd finally be worthy of approval.

But I was running on empty.

Signing up for things, not finishing them, and barely keeping up with the rest of my life.

The answer is simple:
Stop talking about it.
Stop seeking approval from everyone else.

Talk the talk and walk the walk

Choose yourself, stop talking and **start doing** what's best for you.

No one else needs to understand, and that's okay.

When you stop talking and start listening, you'll see exactly what to do next.

If you're feeling stuck, wanting to do better—**take action.**
Don't wait for perfect clarity.
Don't wait for the "right time."

The perfect time doesn't exist. Just jump. ***Just do it.***

Overthinking is a dream killing regret machine.
—don't let it consume the one chance you have to live the life you desire, not everyone gets the opportunity.

Your first thought or feeling is your intuition.

Listen to it.

If you allow overthinking to kick in, you will second-guess everything. Every. Single. Time.

Try this instead.
Think about all the good that could happen instead of focusing on worse-case-scenarios.

Self-sabotage?
If that were an Olympic sport, I'd have a gold medal in every category:

Avoidance
Procrastination
Perfectionism
—you name it. I mastered it.

But here's the truth:
Self-sabotage doesn't mean you're broken. It just means you're holding onto fears from the past that don't define who you are today.

It's okay *to feel scared or have fear of the unknown.*

But that fear?

It doesn't get to control your life anymore.
Because you no longer allow it to.

Perfectionism
is fear with a
Pinterest board.
Pretty doesn't mean
it's powerful.
Ship the damn thing.

Chapter 3

Breaking the Cycle

Even If Your Hands Shake While You Do It

So, now you see it—the patterns, the cycles, the sabotage.

Coolio.
Let's talk about what happens next... before you try to talk yourself out of this whole damn thing.

When I realized I was standing in my own way, I took a long, hard look at my daily life.
—and holy shit, it was a slow burn disaster.

I was working too much—12-hour days at least. In the evening, I numbed out on alcohol and doom-scrolled into oblivion. Then I'd fall into zombie-numb-out-mode and that was my norm, *just so I could shut everything off.*

I'd eat whatever I could find—make a "girl dinner" or nothing at all—**then pass out**. I'd wake up hung over, feeling like shit with barely any sleep, and repeat the cycle.

I couldn't keep up with groceries.
I couldn't keep up with chores.

I damn sure couldn't keep up with fully taking care of myself.

That was the cycle, day after day.

And deep down, I knew if I didn't break it and make small, steady changes.
—I'd burn out for good.

So I did what felt almost too simple:
I started with less.

Micro-Shifts = Real Change

Here's what most people miss about growth:
They aim too big, too fast.

By setting massive goals that feel so far out of reach—it's almost easier to sabotage right out of the gate than trying.

It can feel like an endless loop until you zoom out and see the bigger picture.

Craving more opportunities?
Stronger relationships?
Owning your own business?
Living a peaceful AF life?

Whatever it is, dream big.

But in the meantime, start where you actually are and set yourself up for success that lasts.

Yes, the goal is there, but start with smaller milestones.
—or you're gonna quit and sabotage yourself before you even start.

Start a goal to save $500 each month, not $1,000.
Go to bed 30 minutes earlier.
Drink two more glasses of water.
Spend more time outside.

Set yourself up to actually reach the goal and celebrate every single win. It gives you something concrete to work toward, without feeling overwhelmed.

I decided it was time to cut my hours back where I could.

Working 12 hours a day was a choice.
—not something anyone had asked me to do, even though the workload was impossible for one person—and they knew it.

I was constantly overworking myself because I thought I had to.

But in reality?
I had my regular shift, unless extra time was requested.
—but I was already grinding, so no one bothered or they'd use intimidation and passive aggressive behavior with me.

So, I started setting boundaries around work.

I gave myself permission to leave when my shift was over and actually start taking lunch breaks. *No extra hours just to please everyone else.*

Once I started cutting back at work, I realized I had more time to take care of myself.

Food?

Suddenly, I had time to cook decent meals. I started going to bed earlier, drinking in moderation, cleaning up my eating habits, and moving my body.

I started a "dancing in my kitchen" daily challenge, picked up pilates again and started taking more walks with my little one, Scout Elizabeth

Just allowing myself to feel again.

It felt like the most basic changes, but they were game changers. I cut back on social media and shut the damn TV off—**that was a huge shift too.**

I could see that I was wasting so much time doom scrolling, consuming everyone else's energy and opinions instead of focusing on my own well-being.

That was huge for me—***getting rid of distractions meant the clearer my mind became.***

I realized I wasn't avoiding things as much anymore.

I wasn't hiding behind the alcohol, the 12-hour workdays, or the phone screen.

I've been making these changes for some time now. —*learning new things and expanding my mind by looking at the bigger picture.*

The difference is like night and day.

These weren't huge, drastic changes.
They were little steps I could sustain.

Truth Bomb:
Small Steps Build Big Dreams

Drink more water.
Eat healthier.
Get more rest.
Move your body.
Say no to BS.

The goal isn't to be a superhero.
The goal is to stop self-destructing.

Stop Pretending You Don't Know

Let's be real—most of us already know what's keeping us caught in a loop.

We just don't want to face it.
I sure AF didn't wanna face my bullshit, but I'm grateful I did and continue to practice mindfulness each day.

I had some dark coping mechanisms—*like a crutch to avoid facing my reality.*

I had to admit I was saying yes to everything because I didn't want to feel replaceable.

I had to admit I was scared to slow down because I thought it meant I was lazy.

But here's the thing:
You can be healing and high-functioning.
You can be productive and still be a fucking mess inside.

So I slowed down.
I started feeling.
I got uncomfortable.

And that's when things started changing.

Nervous System 101 (Without the Fluff)

Your nervous system isn't just a concept for yoga teachers or trauma therapists—*it's your body's operating system.*

If you're constantly in fight-or-flight, you'll always default to coping—*whether that's with alcohol, overworking, doom-scrolling, rage-cleaning, ghosting people, numbing out, or whatever your personal crutch is.*

There's nothing wrong with you.

These aren't random habits—they're your nervous system screaming, *"I don't feel safe."*

So we regulate—not through perfection, but through patterns.

It feels weird at first.
But weird isn't wrong. It's just unfamiliar.

You're not failing.
You're rewiring.

TAKE CARE
OF YOUR
MIND

The Power of Moderation & Accountability

Here's something I had to learn the hard way:
like it or not, moderation is actually an incredibly huge key to clearing your mind and changing your life.

Whether it's drinking alcohol or scrolling on your phone, *balance is everything.*

We're all having our own human experience—some days, you'll have too many drinks, doom-scroll for hours, or skip your walk.

That's totally okay.

The real work is about being accountable to yourself.

It's about recognizing when you're slipping back into old patterns and consciously making the choice to shift it.

Perfection? Not realistic.
But awareness and intention?
That's where it's at, that's the real flex.

New day = new mindset = new opportunities

Shifting Self-Talk & Getting Real
With Your Inner Critic

One of the biggest changes I had to make was the way I talked to myself.

So many of us don't realize how damaging our inner dialogue can be.

That little voice that tells you you're not doing enough? **Yeah—it's time to check that tone.**

If you keep telling yourself you're a mess, a screw-up, or not capable—guess what?

Your subconscious is taking notes, saying:
"Saweeeet! Let's keep finding evidence to prove that's true."

You are the creator of your reality and your mind will believe what you tell it.

(It also believes shady narratives we don't even realize are playing "catch me if you can" on repeat in there too.)

Repetition becomes programming.

Programming becomes your life.

You don't need 100 affirmations.

Start with one:
"I'm doing better."

Say it to yourself in the mirror.

Yes, even if it feels silly as hell.
—even when you look like you've been hit by a hangover from 1995.

Say it when your hands are shaking.
Say it when you don't believe it yet.

Eventually—you will.

Move on:
Break the Pattern, on purpose.

Change feels uncomfortable because you're breaking a pattern—***a cycle that's familiar but not healthy.***

It's time to get uncomfortable on purpose.

You don't have to get everything right.
*You just have to stop getting it wrong—**on purpose.***

Once you're aware of the patterns, make the choice to change it.

If you don't like something, ***change it.***

If you don't like how you're talking to yourself, ***stop doing it.***

Be conscious.
Be aware.
Take action.

You've already started. Now it's time to keep going.

But more importantly—once you start seeing your nervous system as part of this process, everything starts clicking.

You're not coping with old habits anymore.
—you're thriving.

You can keep living in the same loop because it's familiar...

> ***Or you can break free—on purpose.***
> ***Even if your hands shake while you do it.***

No one said it would be easy.
But I promise you—it will be worth it.

You don't change your life by white-knuckling it.

You change it by giving yourself wins you can actually reach.

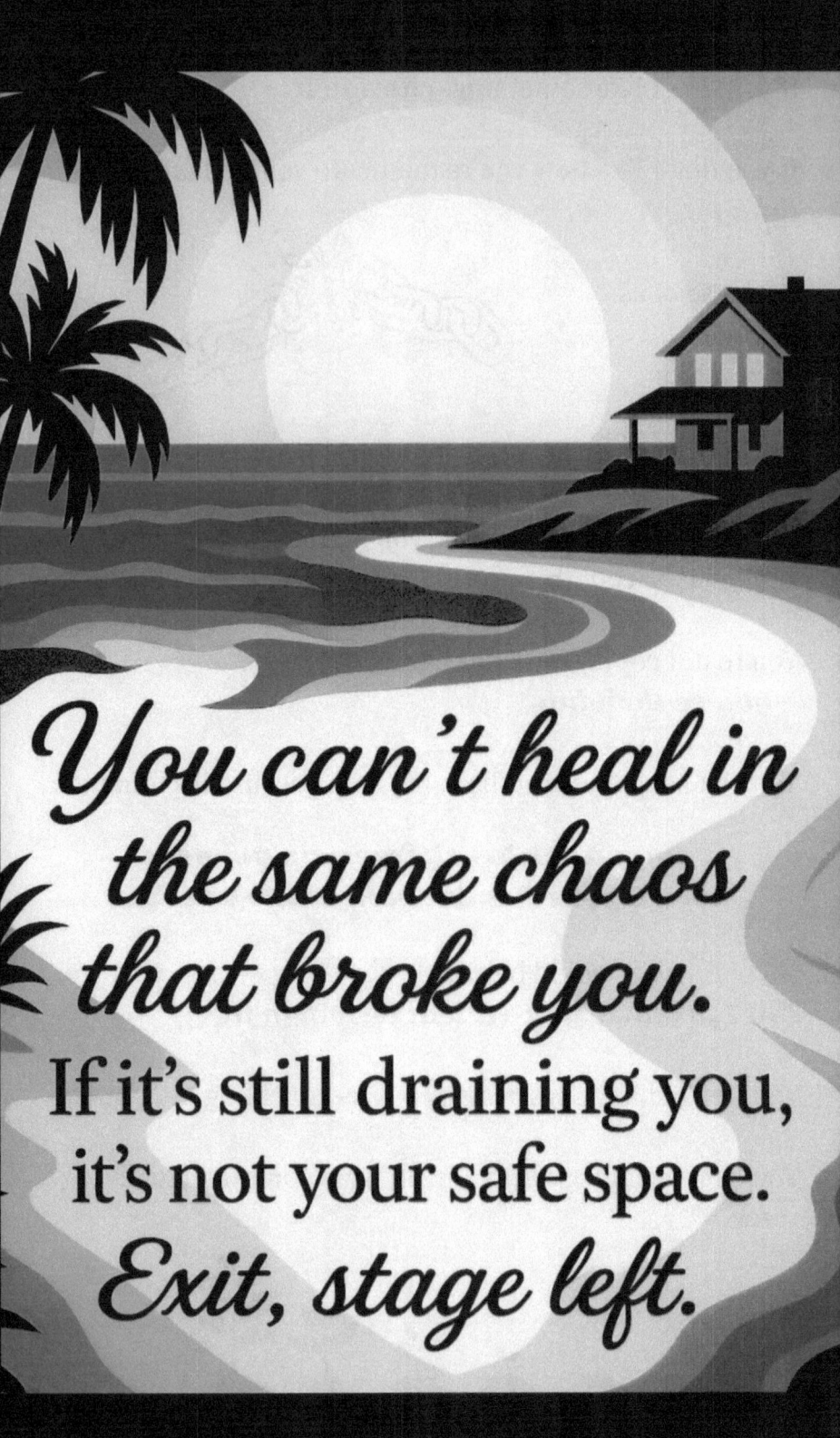

You can't heal in
the same chaos
that broke you.
If it's still draining you,
it's not your safe space.
Exit, stage left.

Chapter 4

Fear Can Throw on Fresh Kicks & a Full-Blown Attitude

Let It Simmer TF Down in the Backseat

Fear is part of the process. **Period**.

It's not going away—*but it sure as hell doesn't get to drive anymore.*

This isn't about kicking fear out. It's about telling it:
"Sit your twitchy ass down, buckle up, and zip it."

You're not exorcising fear—you're learning how to cohabitate with it without giving it access to the AUX cord or letting it DJ the whole damn party anymore.

This is about moving with fear, even when it's loud, sweaty, and wearing a knockoff confidence costume.

Courage Looks Chaotic—And That's the Point

Here's the truth:
Courage is just fear dressed up in a dope outfit with a fucking plan.

It's not clean or perfect—it's chaotic, brave AF, and still showing up.

Some of my loudest, most obnoxious fears?

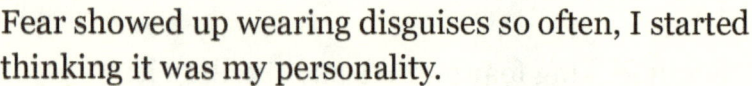

- Judgment
- Being "too much" or "not enough"
- Saying the wrong thing
- *Saying the real thing*
- Sharing my messy-as-hell truth
- Failing in public
- Succeeding—then freezing because I had no damn clue what to do next.

Fear showed up wearing disguises so often, I started thinking it was my personality.

The more I showed up anyway, the more I realized:
People judged me regardless.

Shit still fell apart.

I still said cringeworthy things.
And guess what? I survived.

In fact... I leveled TF up.
Life got real. Life got better.

Because walking with fear taught me what its real purpose was—protection.

Clumsy, outdated, overdramatic protection.
—like a chihuahua in a thunder vest with a hammer trying to guard a castle.

But protection nonetheless.

So I stopped fighting it.

I learned to nod at it, pat it on the head, and say:
"Thanks bro, but I've got this."

They're Gonna Judge You—Do It Anyway

Everyone's got their own filters, traumas, projections, and Netflix-binge-worthy personal baggage.

People will judge you. That's part of the human experience.

But the minute you stop letting their imaginary opinions of you become your navigation system?

That's when the real freedom shows up.

Letting go of fear isn't about recklessness—*it's about being rooted.*

Rooted in the truth that your growth is yours.
Your healing, your pacing, your timing, your techniques.

You don't owe a soul an explanation for how you choose to rise. There will always be people who judge your decisions.

No one knows what you went through and the choices you had to make.

FREE
your
mind

There will always be people who support and encourage you every step of the way.
—those are the ones to focus on and keep close.

And the ones who judge your process?
They might just be the ones who haven't started their own.

And that's okay—you're not doing any of this for them. You're doing it for you.

Other People's Noise ≠ Your Truth

They might still be sitting in their own loop.
—stuck, overwhelmed, unsure how to begin.

And when you get to a place of understanding that everyone is just trying to figure it out, you stop needing their approval.

We all have our own stories.
Our own pasts.
Our own fears in disguise.

And that's the incredible thing about staying in your lane.
—you get to be in charge of your day-to-day life, just like everyone else.

You get to choose what decisions and moves you make along the way.

You choose.
You decide.

So, don't waste your energy wondering what people might be saying or thinking.

They're probably just trying to survive, get out and stay out of their own mental prison, just like you. Just like me.

And yes—some of them are judging.
That's reality.

But if we assume that judgment is always aimed at us, we miss the point.

Everyone is dealing with their own fear, their own hesitation, their own *"Am I doing this right?"* rerun.

If they're critiquing your path, it's probably because they haven't committed to their own.

And that's their story—not yours.

You Wouldn't Imagine It If You Weren't Capable of It

Fear hits especially hard when we're stepping into something new.

A new business.
A new relationship.
A new version of ourselves.

You start prepping and planning, then suddenly your brain starts whispering:

"Can I actually do this?"
"Is it too good to be true?"

That's where most people stop and jump on the self sabotage dream killing bandwagon.

Again, here's the thing—if you can imagine it, that means you have the capacity for it.

You wouldn't have the idea if it wasn't already living somewhere inside you.

That's your sign:
You're ready.

Even if you're shaking like a shorkie on espresso.
—you're still doing it.

Readiness isn't a damn feeling—it's a choice, it's a decision.

And that's not small.
That's rebellious.
That's radical.
That's legacy-level bold.

That's the kind of bold your future self will thank you for later.

The Fear of Follow-Through Is a Thing
And You're Not Alone

Will I ghost my goals?
Will I fuck up my own success again?
Yup. I've been there too.

I've made plans so incredible they belonged on Pinterest...
only to burn out before I ever launched a damn thing.

It wasn't laziness. It was freeze-mode.

The kind of functional perfectionism that wears a blazer
and goes to therapy but still refuses to let you start
anything.

I thought I needed to be fully healed, fully prepared, and
fully everything before I made moves.

Plot twist?
That's a lie fear sells when it's scared of your potential.

Sometimes Healing Is Just a Damn Pause

Sometimes healing isn't a process.
It's a pause.
A breath.

A choice to just "be" for a second without dissecting every
damn feeling under a microscope.

Anxiety, overthinking, over planning, coping.
—*it doesn't mean you're broken. It means your system is trying to keep you safe the only way it knows how.*

But now, you get to teach it a new way.

Talk to Yourself Like Someone Worth Saving

Start talking to yourself out loud.
Unapologetically.
In the car. In the kitchen. In the middle of aisle five.

If someone catches you mid-monologue?

Smile and say: "I'm just in a meeting with my inner badass."

Because when you pause and say: *"Hey—I'm okay right now. I've got this. I don't have to stay in overdrive and be perfect before I can rest"*

You're rewriting the damn manual and self-talk plays a pivotal role.

Confidence Comes After the Scary Thing

Sometimes the most powerful thing you can do is notice.
That's not weird. That's wisdom.

Name the fear. Hold it. But don't let it spiral you out.

Confidence isn't the launchpad.
—*it's the side effect.*

It doesn't walk in before the scary thing.

It shows up after you've done it shaking, sweating, second guessing—*but you did it anyway.*

It's something you learn, something you build.

So, let fear ride shotgun if it must.

Just let it wear those fresh kicks and throw shade from the backseat.

Because, baby — you're the one driving now.

Fear's a liar with a great wardrobe.

Stop falling for the costume changes. You're the main character now.

Chapter 5

Celebrate Every Single Win Like You Built Rome

Because You Did. And You're Not Asking for Permission.

Okay, I've seen the patterns and stopped letting fear drive...
Now what?

I realized I had trust issues with myself by way of overthinking.

The nonstop loop of second-guessing decisions I'd already made—***or hadn't even made yet.***

Worrying if I hurt someone.
Wondering if they misunderstood me.
Worrying if I was too much or not enough.
Again.

But check this out.

Worrying and wondering can show up as fucked up ways of actually worshiping the problem itself.

Be aware.
Listen closely.
Course Correct.

You are the creator of your reality and your mind will believe what you tell it. ***Every. Damn. Time.***

Live with Intention.
Not Perfection.

Here's what I know now.
I live my life with intention. Not perfection.

I don't go out of my way to hurt anyone.
I do my best to be aware.
I do my best to be kind.
I do my best to communicate & still honor my own needs.

We all have different perspectives, different struggles, different needs, different triggers, different stories.

It's literally impossible to be understood by everyone all the time—***especially by those committed to misunderstanding you.***

You can't pause your growth to protect someone else's comfort zone.

Enabling unhealthy behavior is still self sabotage.
No matter the circumstance or situation.

Self-Trust Starts Small

That shift—from worry to trust—didn't happen with some big breakthrough.

It happened with small-ass promises I actually kept to myself.

Like:

- Getting up and eating breakfast
- Taking a morning walk
- Sending the damn emails I kept putting off
- Grocery shopping even when I didn't feel safe in public

These might sound small to someone else, but to me?
They were the foundation of rebuilding.

Those micro-wins?

I celebrated the hell out of them.

Didn't get everything done?
Nope, and that's okay.

But I did something.
And that something meant I wasn't avoiding it.

I wasn't ghosting my own growth.

One Goal: Avoid Avoiding

So, I shrunk my to-do list down to one goal each day:
Avoid avoiding.

That was it, the shift.

Don't let your brain spiral.
Catch it. Don't stall out.

Just do the next thing that feels right—**even if it's tiny.**
Even if it's awkward.
Even if you're scared.

That's how new habits are born.
That's how you slowly start believing in yourself again.

That's how you show your brain:
"I got this and I got me."

Eventually, you don't have to hype yourself up to move.
You just do it.

Because it feels good. Because it's part of who you are now.

The "I'm Too 'Unsexy'" Side of Growth

Living your growth doesn't always look bangin'.
Sometimes it's just:

- Drinking more water
- Eating better food
- Stretching
- Shutting off the fucking TV
- Saying no to plans and yes to silence
- Walking away from what's draining
- Saying no to things that keep people-pleasing mode locked and loaded
- Saying no to things out of your control. ***Period.***

The Layoff and the Lie

When I was laid off, the first thing I thought was:
"I need to start applying for jobs."

Because that's the programming, right?
Do what's safe.
Do what society says.
Get back on someone's payroll.
Sit at a desk and prove you're useful.

Hustle

But every time I pictured it, I felt sick.
Like... physically sick.

I went to interviews. I crushed them.

All of the changes I had made prepped me to get farther
than I ever had before—***and I'm grateful for those
opportunities every day.***

But in my gut, I knew—this wasn't it.
I was performing. Smiling. Nodding.

Meanwhile, my soul was screaming:
"This ain't the move—set me free."

So I listened to that scream.
I listened to my body.
I listened to my intuition. Closely.

freedom

I kept creating, writing, learning, growing.

I opened up space to build something real—**for me.
For my kids. For my legacy.**

And even when I wasn't sure how it would work out, I had peace.

Real, deep, centered peace that I'd never had in my life.

That's Alignment. That's Self-Trust.
It's not loud. It's not flashy. But it's solid.

So yeah—celebrate the win when you send that one email.

Celebrate the win when you finally eat a real meal.

Celebrate the win when you don't overthink something to death.

Celebrate Every Single Win Like You Built Rome.
Because you did.
And you're not asking for permission.

Overthhinking is just self-sabotage with spreaalsheets. Close the tabs. Make a move

Analysis paralysis isn't sexy.

Chapter 6
Choose Yourself Again and Again

You made it.

You didn't just read a book—you met yourself in these pages.

And you kept going.

Through the noise.
Through the patterns.
Through the damn resistance.
You looked at the hard stuff most people avoid.

That says a lot.

If you're reading this eBook or holding the print version in your hands right now, **it means you know it's time to stop playing small.**

Time to stop pretending you don't feel the disconnect.

Time to stop self-sabotaging the delicious life you actually want and deserve.

You don't have to be fearless.

It's about getting loyal AF to your future self.
—to the point that fear gets bored and stops showing up…for good.

This isn't about never doubting again.

It's about recognizing when you're sliding back into old habits—**and choosing to redirect yourself anyway, even if it feels uncomfortable.**

But now the good shit begins:
Integration. Embodiment. Action.

Where to Go From Here

This book isn't the end.
It's a beginning—the first of many.

The truth is, transformation isn't a one-and-done moment.

It's a series of moments where you make the choice to do things differently.

To stop overthinking.
To stop people-pleasing.
To start living with your whole self at the table.

And if you're ready for that? I'm here for it.

I created this book as a spark—*but I've also built space for the fire to grow.*

If you're seeking support that feels like a real conversation and not another "five-step funnel to success".
—*here's how we can keep moving forward together.*

Wanna dive deeper, stay in the loop and get real-life tools?

Explore my private coaching and wellness community for updates, mindset drops, and the occasional spicy rant at:

www.caliaymee.com

Yes, it's a vibe. Bring snacks.

Need more clarity before getting started?

Reach out and book a free 15-minute call to chat more with me: **amy@caliaymee.com**

This work is personal—and so is your next step.

You're Not Broken.
You're Not Behind.
You don't need more time to prove you're ready.

Nobody's coming to save you.
You don't need to be saved.
You just need you.

Choose yourself.
Again.
And again.
And again.

Because at the end of the day, you are your own greatest project.

And if you need permission—this is it.

The magic is already in motion.
Let's keep going.
You've already started.

You don't owe anyone access to the old version of you that barely survived.

Sending you love and light, always,

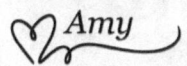 *Amy*

Follow my journey...
@caliaymee | www.caliaymee.com

Waiting until you're 'ready' is just another way of procrastinating, but with a pretty bow on top

Thank You for Reading

Thank you for riding shotgun with me through my first book. Writing it wasn't just about telling a little bit about my story.

It's a torch. A signal flare.
A wink that says you're not alone.

It's about you, the person who's ready to move forward, even if it feels messy sometimes.

If this lit a spark in that wild heart of yours
—then hell to the yes.
That's the beginning of the fire.

Stay loud. Stay weird. Stay curious. Stay bold.
Own your voice and rock your edges.

And for the love of all that's holy, don't shrink now.

Stay in your fucking power.
We're just getting started.

Sending you love and light, always,
Amy ♡

About the Author

Amy Nozicka is a wellness and lifestyle improvement coach known for blending deep wisdom with no BS real talk. Her work is all about self-trust, transformation, and showing up in your life—loudly, boldly, and unapologetically.

After surviving through some brutal chapters—including toxic dynamics, quiet self-sabotage, and that sneaky thing called corporate burnout, Amy decided to rewrite her own story. One choice at a time, she built a life of intentional freedom, showing how to break the cycles that keep us small.

She's not just an author—she's an artist, a truth-slinger, and a lighthouse for anyone ready to burn the rulebook and live from the inside out.

When she's not writing, painting or coaching, you can catch her behind the wheel of her M4 convertible, Daezeee, chasing sunsets down the PCH, doing handstands on the beach, inking her story into her skin, or making waves (literally) along the California coast.

This book is part of her truth.
The rest? She's still writing it.

Follow Amy's journey:
www.caliaymee.com

www.ingramcontent.com/pod-product-compliance
Lightning Source LLC
Chambersburg PA
CBHW031257120626
46545CB00007B/2858